"How Can God Use This for His Glory?"

"How Can God Use This for His Glory?"

Linda Bennett

Copyright © 2009 by Linda Bennett.

Library of Congress Control Number: 2009900101
ISBN: Hardcover   978-1-4415-0147-9
               Softcover   978-1-4415-0146-2

All rights reserved. No part of this book may be reproduced or transmitted in any form or by any means, electronic or mechanical, including photocopying, recording, or by any information storage and retrieval system, without permission in writing from the copyright owner.

This book was printed in the United States of America.

To order additional copies of this book, contact:
Xlibris Corporation
1-888-795-4274
www.Xlibris.com
Orders@Xlibris.com
54657

Contents

Acknowledgements 9

Introduction 13

Chapter One
Wait a minute, what just Happened? 15

Chapter Two
A little History 17

Chapter Three
Is it really True? 28

Chapter Four
The other side of the Fence 37

Chapter Five
God Reached out to Me 39

Chapter Six
How can God use me Again? 43

Chapter Seven
Overcoming Mountains 48

Chapter Eight
Missing a chance to help my Brother 55

Chapter Nine
Stepping back into Life   58

Chapter Ten
Nothing is going to happen to you without going through me First!   64

Chapter Eleven
I don't deserve This!   67

Chapter Twelve
Still Overwhelming!   70

Chapter Thirteen
Unchained!   75

Epilogue   81

Bibliography   85

Dedication

This book is dedicated to two couples:

The first couple is one I have never met, nor do I know their names. Years ago, they lost a two-year-old son in a tragic accident. I don't know the details of the accident. I can not imagine their immense pain and grief. But in spite of pain and tragedy, they reached out and agreed to donate their son's heart to one they had never met nor knew
the details about.

The one who benefited from their action is one I love, my niece, Taylor. When she was three, a virus attacked her heart and she needed a heart transplant.

Our family has been blessed to watch Taylor grow into a vibrant young lady. When I look at her, I want so much to wrap my arms around the couple and tell them how much their action benefited another.

In this book, the question is asked,
"How can God use this for His glory?"
I may never see with my own eyes or hear
with my own ears how the tragedy that befell
me is going to be used for His glory, but
I know it can happen.
Just looking at Taylor, I know it can happen!

The other couple is Steve and Barb Vanderlaan.

Steve and Barb go to the Williamston Free
Methodist Church. I learned that not long
before I came to the church, they lost a son
in a tragic accident. I didn't believe Steve
and Barb would even talk to someone like me,
with the history I have. But not only did they
talk to me; they have prayed with me,
they have laughed with me, and they have
even cared for me when I was sick. How God
used them in my life strengthened me in
many ways. I am grateful for their friendship,
for God used them to show me Himself.

Acknowledgements

My Family

Many Friends
Brittany Anderson
Melissa Andres
Paula Barbee
Judy Bennett
Mark & Lorrie Boyce
Judy Bristley
Tom and Berta Case
Jan Cleeton
Joel & Erica Close
Jan Close
Lacy Davis
Ron & Jackie Fernelius
Bill & Carolyn Fitzpatrick
Bob & Debbie Fowler
Carla Funk
Liz Hurd
Cindy Jacobs
Janet Kissling
Erwin & Alma Krueger
Linda Krueger
Ken & Stephanie LaBelle

Gary and Alicia Lucious
Gary Messenger
Jackie Mueller
Cody & Keisha Plaskett
Dennie Plumb
Judy Shinabarger
Jason & Jodi Spaulding
Vicki Teed
Nancy Thornhill
Kim Volz & Sally Woodward-Volz
The Friend I am Forgetting To Mention

My Pastors & their Wives
Pastor David & Diane Bowser
Pastor Doug & Kathy Bradshaw
Pastor Scott & Michele Durbin
Pastor Roger & Sheryl Allen
Pastor Phil & Emily Owen
Pastors John & Linda Waldo
Pastor Bruce & Gina Lawton

The Congregations' of
The Linden Free Methodist Church
The West Flint Church of the Nazarene
The Williamston Free Methodist Church
New Covenant Ministries, Free Methodist Church

My Professionals' Advisors
Ambrose Rehabilitation and Counseling:
Elizabeth Piner, Julie, & Deb
Dr. Henry Hagenstien
Dr. Stephen Harrison
Dr. Heidi Johnson and Staff

Brad Lockwood, Attorney-at-Law, and Dave
(Brad's Assistant)
Dr. Roy Meland
Dr. Jesse Soulia
Dr. Rick Smith & Staff
Matthew Syzek
Carol Van Drie, Author
Marge Peska, Nutritionist,
Sparrow Health Systems
Lansing-West Saginaw Meijer Pharmacy Staff
Genesee County Free Medical Clinic, Staff,
Volunteers & In memory of Rose Davies

My Teammates at Peckham Inc.:
You are my hero's!
"I may have a disability, but my disability
doesn't have me!"

And to Mary, although we encountered similar situations we prayed to God for His intervention. I know your still healing, as I am. Let's not give up the fight. God has forgiven us, the families have forgiven us, let's forgive ourselves, and let Him use the tragedies that came into our lives for His glory!

Last But Not Least
In Loving Memory of My Mom:
Nancy Sue Price

All profits from the production of this book will be designated for non-profit & charitable organizations.

Introduction

I am on my way to my sister's home, for she has invited me for dinner! I am running a little late-three years, one month, and two hours, to be exact. I didn't take a wrong turn or forget where I was going. Instead of hitting a bump on the road of life, I ran into a crater. My family won't notice I am so late, not that they lost track of me or I of them. I won't mention it to them or make a big deal out of being so late. No apologies will be needed or understood. To them, today is a day to get together to eat, fish, and have some fun. It is for me as well; but it is also a day where I can pick up where I started three years, one month, and two hours ago. That day, so long ago, seems like yesterday in my mind, and a day I will never be able to forget. I will look back to that day as the day my world stopped turning, but the rest of the world continued to turn—the day I was stuck in a crater with what was left of my faith in God.

To understand, you will need to bear with me as I recall, to the best of my recollection, the crater itself and how I had to pull and push, all the while kicking and screaming, my way out of that crater—the one that made me so late for dinner.

Chapter One

Wait a minute, what just Happened?

Waking up in the hospital emergency room again! Another seizure? Dazed and confused; I was trying to get my brain back on line. My brother Tom and my Pastor, David Bowser, were standing next to my bed. I was trying to figure out where I went off-line. Bits and pieces started to come together, May 29, 2004, just a normal Saturday. I had called my sister, Sue, who had invited me to come to her house for dinner. The last thing I remember was driving down the road, deciphering which would be the best way to get to her home from where I was.

But as I lay on the gurney in the emergency room, little by little, it started to occur to me that something bad had happened, but I couldn't put my finger on it. As Tom and Pastor David stood next to me, a state trooper came in and told me I had been involved in a car accident. My mind was numb, for I had no memory of any accident. He then stated my car had hit another car from the rear, and the man in the other car did not survive. I immediately looked at my brother and pastor, two men I loved and respected, looking for an affirmation that what the state trooper had said was not true. But their silence confirmed the horror. I felt like I couldn't breathe. I wondered if I was in a nightmare where I was going to wake up at any moment. But it kept going; I couldn't wake up. I couldn't believe it had really happened. The state trooper said they would need to take a blood test to show I was not under the influence of any drugs or alcohol and I would need to have a relative sign the papers as well as myself, giving permission for tests to be done. I looked at Tom and asked if he would sign. I remember him signing the paper and then the poke of the needle. They put the tubes in a special bag, one I have never seen before. I realized then that I was being investigated for a criminal action.

The next thing I remember about that evening was when one of my best friends, whose name is also Linda, standing next to my bed. As my nervous system gave into the overwhelming occurrences of the evening, I began to shake uncontrollably. Thinking of how God had used me in so many ways to reach out to people in the past, I was so confused. I looked Linda in the eyes and asked with all humility, "How can God use this for His glory?" *To her credit, she remained silent.*

Chapter Two

A little History

I thought I was done with seizures. The first one I had, which was witnessed by others, was on May 27, 2002. It started as a great day. It was Memorial Day weekend, and I had plans to spend time with my family. Within a half hour of arriving at my stepsister's home for the day, we were eating dinner, and I was enjoying seeing my nieces and nephews fishing in the lake and playing around the yard. The last thing I remember was talking with my aunt.

The next thing I knew, I was in the emergency room at the hospital, where my older brother, Tom, and my older sister, Sue, were assuring the physician I didn't do drugs or drink alcoholic beverages. From my perspective, it took a few minutes to realize something terrible had happened to me. I remember very few details of that afternoon. I do remember not feeling well and being attached to several machines, including oxygen and IVs, along with having to have numerous tests, including a CT scan and an MRI. I also remember my father coming in with tears in his eyes and stating, "I am the one who should die first!"

It was then I realized, from my family's perspective, the day of food, fun, and fishing had turned into a day of horror for them. Apparently, they noticed at one point that I was not paying attention, staring off into space. My body then stiffened up and my face began to turn blue and then purple. Their first thoughts were that I was choking, and then that I was having a heart attack. They immediately called for an ambulance, and my brother and sister tried to do mouth-to-mouth resuscitation, but my mouth would not open. When the ambulance arrived, the paramedics assured my family I was breathing but unconscious.

I was admitted to the hospital where I was put in a padded bed and was told I couldn't get out of bed without assistance. The medicine I was on made me feel terrible. I was told that I had suffered a grand mal seizure. The doctors were unsure as to why I had the seizure, so they wanted to observe me for a few days.

Immediately I started to ask God why this was happening and how in the world I was going to get through this. I was already on unemployment and looking for a job. Now in the hospital, I was unable to work, which made me ineligible for unemployment benefits because you have to be able to work to do so. I also did not have medical insurance and knew the hospital bill would be in the thousands of dollars. I had no idea how I was going to make ends meet.

The day following the grand mal seizure, I had a visit from a neurologist who had been assigned to me. Without introducing himself or telling me any other information, he announced I could not drive for six months. He then left my room. Already not feeling well, I became overwhelmed and wasn't quite sure what to do with this information. I later found out that some states have laws that prohibit those who have seizures from driving for a certain amount of time after a seizure. Michigan law states six months. Other states have different timetables; some don't have any at all. I wanted to move! All kinds of things went through my head; how in the world was I going to make it with no job, no money, and being unable to drive?

I was overwhelmed, but immediately my family and friends started to reach out and assist me in many ways. Linda, who is a registered nurse, knew there were programs that hospitals had to help people who don't have insurance. She actually gathered the forms for me, filled them out, held my hand to help me sign them, and then turned them in for me.

The doctors never found out why I had the seizure. I was released five days later into my sister's care. My family made plans for me to stay at my sister's home for at least two weeks so I could have constant supervision. This was a great challenge to me, for I was used to living a life of an independent, single person. I did have a brief period, over thirteen years ago, following a car accident in which I had suffered a severe head injury and several broken bones, for which my sister took care of me during that time as well. But, other than that, I had always been able to care for myself, was active, and had traveled the world doing various missions. But now I needed help again, and things were up in the air as to why, when, and where my next seizure was going to happen.

In a couple of weeks, I was able to move around, though not my normal self because of the medicine my body was adjusting to. I tried to do all I could to care for myself. People from my home church, which at the time was the Linden Free Methodist Church, took up an offering on my behalf. The offering covered not only my rent for June but also my car payment. A few days later, the ladies from the Deeper Life Retreat Committee, which I chaired, took up an offering for me, which helped me cover all the other bills for my household for that first month. Right away, out of thanksgiving to the Lord, I tithed on all the monetary gifts I received. Many may not agree with tithing on such gifts, but I wanted to; I was in awe at how God was providing for me. People from all over sent me cards of encouragement, many with monetary gifts enclosed. I was able to pay my monthly bills, which included my rent, car payment, utilities, phone, and credit card debt, which I had been working for over three years to eliminate.

I started to receive bills from the hospital. *Big bills*! I tried not to panic, but as the bills started to pile up, it was harder not to be overwhelmed. The bills totaled around $1,400. A friend stepped in and said she felt God leading her to pay those bills for me. Again, I was in awe. I called the hospital because I had not yet received the big bill. I found out they had no record of my application for financial help. After making arrangements with my sister for transportation, I went to the hospital and met with the lady I spoke with on the phone. She asked me a few questions and said she would get back with me after she talked to her boss. A few days later she called me and told me the bill had been take care of, "paid in full"!

God continued to provide through gifts from friends or by providing odd jobs I was able to do, such as house-sitting and caring for people's pets. I even had a couple of opportunities to stay with teenagers as their parents needed to go away for a weekend or a few days. A teen, I felt, could handle a seizure; a dog would just lie down next to me until I came out of one. No matter how much money people gifted me with, I always tithed on the money God paid me through these jobs. It was amazing to me how God was never late on providing the money for me to pay any of my bills that were due.

Although I was not able to drive, God provided again and again as people would call and ask if I could come and help them; coming to pick me up was never a big deal. Even when I needed to go somewhere, such as a doctor's appointment or other places, God would provide for me to have transportation.

I had many setbacks because I continued to have seizures. I never knew when I was going to have one. Some people who experience seizures have what is called an *aura*, which is some type of feeling or a trigger, such as a shaky hand, that lets them know they are about to have a seizure. I have never experienced an aura that I know of.

If I have, I don't remember after a seizure that I did. I have had those are called *grand mal,* where I fall down, shake, don't breathe, and unfortunately foam at the mouth. I have also had what are called *petit mal seizures*, which can range from staring at something for a long time to putting my head down as if I were taking a nap. I don't remember anything during the seizures, and I am very confused for a while after I come out of one.

    I even had a seizure while I was shopping for shoes one day. My friend Debbie had taken me to a shoe store to get a good pair of walking shoes since walking was my main source of transportation at the time. She told me to take my time and find the best shoes while she waited in her car. She is a physician's assistant and wanted to study for her relicensing exam. I went into the store and took off my sandals. Realizing I would need a pair of socks, I opened a package of socks with full intention of buying them with the shoes. The next thing I remember was being at the corner of Corunna and Dye roads, very confused as to what and why I was there. Little by little, as my brain started to come back on line, I realized I must have had a seizure, walked out of the store past Debbie, who was studying, and headed toward home. The distance I walked was over one and half miles. I do not know if I stopped for traffic or if traffic stopped for me. In the meantime, Debbie had come into the store to see how I was doing with my shopping. After she and the manager of the store thoroughly searched for me, she called 911. She then got in her car and started looking for me. Jodi, a friend from church, was driving by and saw me. She pulled over and could tell right away there was something wrong. I was very confused and scared, for I felt like I had lost Debbie. Jodi said something to me that stuck with me. "I am not going to leave you until we find Debbie!" As soon as we pulled on to Corunna Road and came to the next intersection, I looked up and noticed the car in front of us was Debbie's. Jodi beeped her car horn and got her attention. We pulled into a nearby parking lot. Debbie called 911 back to let them know she had found me then she checked me over to see if I was okay. I was emotionally shaken up but was so glad that I had found my friend.

The next day, I went to the shoe store again and asked to speak to the manager so I could pay for the socks I had inadvertently walked off with. She said she was happy I was okay, and there was "no charge" for the socks. As I look back at that day, I have always found it funny, in a way, because Debbie did say, "Take your time!"

Every time I had a seizure, my medication dosage needed to be increased; and every time that happened, I felt like I was back in the hospital as my body needed to adjust to the increased dosage. Every time I had a seizure, I had to count six months from that date before I could drive again. Michigan law requires people to be seizure free for six months, I had a seizure in October of 2002 and knew I couldn't drive until March. I was looking forward to March with much anticipation; but then, on January 21, 2003, I was talking on the phone with my friend Lorrie when all of a sudden, I hung up the phone. Lorrie immediately called back, but I didn't answer. Alarmed, she called my neighbor Erica. Erica came to my house and could tell I was having a seizure, a pet mal. She called Lorrie back, and Lorrie then called my friend Linda, the RN. Linda told her I was okay; they couldn't do anything for me, just to watch me. She also prepared them for when I came out of the seizure by telling them I would take it hard emotionally. Once I realized I had another seizure, she was right. I did take it hard! I would have to start from what seemed like square one again, more medicine, and six more months without driving. Throughout those months of waiting and recovering, God reminded me constantly that He was still there by providing for me and taking care of me. Friends would tell me how encouraged they were because of how they could see God working in my life and providing for me.

I continued to get odd jobs on and off, and God continued to provide by having people send me monetary gifts. I was thankful to God for every gift I received.

On July 21, I was able to drive again. It had been six months from my last seizure. It was kind of funny because when I did get all the insurance and plates taken care of and was able to get in my car to go somewhere, I thought about it and truly had no place I really needed to go. I was nervous, after over a year of not driving; but thankfully, like many friends said, it is like riding a bike. I found work through a local school district, working as a paraprofessional. I assisted teachers in their classrooms doing various tasks. I enjoyed working with the kids. But then I was offered a part-time position at my church, which at that time was the West Flint Church of the Nazarene. After I started to have seizures and couldn't drive, I started to attend there because it was next door to my apartment, and I had friends that were already going there. The job was for an administrative assistant, and I took the job while I continued to do odd jobs and looked for full-time work. After fourteen months of being seizure free, it was March 2004. I was doing well. My neurologist, at that time, wanted to decrease the dosage of one of my medicines. I agreed because I wanted to get off any medicine I didn't need. It was a nonseizure medicine, so I didn't think twice about it. He wrote a prescription cutting the dose to half of what I was taking, which now meant I had twice the amount of medicine I needed, so I didn't go to the pharmacy right away. First mistake! A week later, a friend and I were out to dinner. I had driven my car to the restaurant. While we were there, I apparently put my head down, chin to chest, and just sat there for a few minutes. I didn't move or respond to my friend. There was apparently a nurse across the aisle from us who came over and checked my pulse to see if I was breathing. My friend informed her I had a seizure disorder, so the nurse suggested they wait for a few minutes. When I came out of the seizure, I picked up where I left off, not realizing I had just missed about five minutes. My friend didn't tell me I had a seizure until were outside the restaurant. She remembered me telling her how emotional I get after I have one. Once she told me, I was in shock for a moment because I didn't believe it! After fourteen months of being seizure free! I handed her my car keys and told her she would need to drive. The next day, I called my neurologist and he called in another prescription. This one was for another seizure medication I had never taken before, so now I was on two. When I went to the pharmacy, I turned in the written prescription for a week earlier. My pharmacist asked me, "Did you already start this new dosage?" I said, "Yes, a week ago." His eyes rolled up in his head, and with a sigh, he said, "That sudden drop in medication is what caused your seizure. You should have been weaned off it!" Then it made sense. That sudden drop is what threw off my brain. I was relieved, in a way, because for the first time since my seizures began, I could put a finger on why this one happened.

But it happened, and I had to deal with the "no driving for six months issue." At church that night, I was in conversation with others in the kitchen and was telling them about my ordeal. One of the ladies there, who had experienced a seizure a while back, told me if the seizure had to do with a change in medicine, state law doesn't require a waiting time. I looked at her in disbelief, and she pulled out of her briefcase something she had gotten off a state website verifying the information. I remember standing there in unbelief. I was in an "awe" mode. I kept saying to myself, "I don't have to wait? I don't have to wait?" I don't have to wait! "Yahoo" finally came out of my mouth. After years of voluntarily setting my keys aside for six months or longer, I finally had a reason. That reason gave me peace that I was okay and wouldn't be breaking any laws by driving. I never called my doctor to verify with him that it was okay for me to drive, and I never received anything in the mail from the state stating I couldn't drive. So I drove—my second mistake. These two mistakes led me to experience haunting guilt; I now call it the "Woulda, Coulda, Shoulda Syndrome."

Chapter Three

Is it really True?

Fast-forward, May 29, 2004: lying in the emergency room at the hospital. I don't remember seeing the car or remember the ambulance ride to the hospital. I just remember bits and pieces of that night. But it was the night my life turned upside down, and it felt like God had pulled the rug out from underneath me. I was flat on my back, looking up and asking God all kinds of questions. "How are you going to use this for your glory?" was the first question. The second was "Why didn't you take me?" It was my fault; I should have been the one to die, not him. All I had were first-degree burns to my arms from the air bag. I probably had a petit mal seizure, which would have relaxed my whole body, which explains why I didn't receive major injuries; my body was relaxed and not tensed up like during a grand mal.

I tried to return to work after the accident. I didn't make it past the first phone call. I was still working as an administrative assistant for my church. My first day back, I felt like something was different, but I couldn't figure out what.

Nothing had changed in the office. All of the staff was there. But then there was the first phone call. For some reason, as soon as the phone started ringing, my heartbeat increased, and I felt I couldn't breathe. I stared at the phone, not knowing how to answer it. My mind went blank and I became very scared. I can't remember if I answered the phone or if a member of the staff picked it up. I do remember walking into Pastor David's office, telling him I needed to go home. I remember going home scared out of my mind. But I didn't know of what. I went to bed although it was only around eleven o'clock in the morning. I had a migraine headache, was sick to my stomach, and every muscle in my body was aching. I felt like I was screaming on the inside, but no one could hear me, except me. I was scared most of the time, but I didn't know why.

About two weeks after the accident, there was a knock on my door. When I went to the door, a man stood outside the screen, and I greeted him. He then told me his name and told me he was the son of the man who died in the accident. I opened my door to him, and he stepped in. I was unable to speak, and tears were welling up in my eyes as he told me he had come to tell me that he and his family didn't hold anything against me because of the accident. By the time he finished that one sentence, I was crying; and then he said, "I didn't come here to upset you." Then he left. I never said a word; I was speechless. It was when he left that the questions started to come to my mind: "Was he a good man?" "What did he do?" "Did he know Jesus?" and "How is your mom?" Questions flooded my heart and head, but I had no one there to answer them. I had missed an opportunity to reach out and tell one of the victims of this nightmare I had caused how sorry I was, but I missed it. I didn't realize it at the time, but my bout with survivor's guilt was just beginning.

I received a call from the state trooper who had investigated the accident. He informed me the investigation was over and I was able to go and clean out my car. My brothers, Tom and George, and my friend Nancy went with me. It was in a salvage yard in Flint. As we walked through the salvage yard and rounded a corner, there was a demolished tan-colored Chevy Cavalier my brothers started to clean out. As I held on to Nancy, I couldn't believe I survived such a devastating crash and, worst yet, that I didn't remember anything about it. It didn't seem possible or real. But I knew my brothers and Nancy wouldn't have taken me there if it didn't need to be done. But as I held on to Nancy, crying and shaking, it was like the nightmare was starting again and I couldn't wake up. I couldn't stop it, and I felt completely helpless and numb on the inside.

The overwhelming guilt led me to call my friend Paula one afternoon, and I asked her to come over because I needed her help. Once she was there, I handed her a list of things to do. I then told her I had called the state trooper who had investigated the accident and had asked him to come over as well. The list of things to do were things I wanted to be done once my goal was met. My goal for that evening was to get arrested.

Once arrested, I could start paying for the awful mistake I had made. The first item on the list was to call my brother Tom and tell him "not" to bail me out. When the state trooper arrived, I told him the circumstances I felt led to the accident. I told him everything. After I was done, he looked at me and said, "Linda, you did not do this out of malicious intent, the investigation is over and you have not been charged with any crimes." I remember sitting there being numb because I expected to be arrested (I even cleaned my house). Deep down I wanted him to arrest me. Once he left, I looked at Paula and said, "How I am going to pay for this now?"

I knew I needed help, but I didn't know where to go. God seemed distant, but my friends and family were close to me. But I knew I needed some professional help. I made an appointment with a professional counselor and asked my friend Carolyn to go with me. My situation seemed to be above the counselor's head, and I walked out knowing she was not the one that could help me. I tried another counselor and saw him a few times; he diagnosed me with depression, which I did have, but I felt something was missing and I was getting nowhere. Thoughts of suicide came to my mind, and I wrestled with them. I felt I had nothing to live for; the life I had was now lost because of a terrible mistake I had made. But my family and friends were in my thoughts as I contemplated suicide. I wanted to go face-to-face with God and ask Him, "Why?" But I knew to commit suicide would hurt even more people-the ones who were standing next to me and helping me along. I couldn't give in, but I didn't want to go on.

I remember being so mad at God I was walking around my apartment alone, crying, with my hands in the air and saying out loud, "What am I to do now? I can't go back! I can't fix this and neither can you! Why did you let this happen? What am I going to do because I can't trust you anymore?"

I knew I didn't want to go back to the lifestyle I had before I knew Jesus, so I had no choice, even as mad as I was, but to stay with Him and walk on. I can honestly say it was not in joy I walked, but in misery. I felt my God, the one for whom I had invested half of my life into, had abandoned me. But I had no choice other than to continue to walk. I was kicking and screaming at him, but I was also holding His hand; as mad as I was, I was holding His hand. (I believe now He was carrying me, just like the "Footprints in the Sand" poem.)

A name kept coming up as people talked to me and wanted to know how I was doing. I would tell those I trusted that I was seeing a professional Christian counselor. Three times, in three different settings, with three different people they would say this counselor's name, and I would say, "No, not him." After the third time of hearing his name, I called him and asked if he would see me. It was a turning point. He had a doctorate in psychology and had more experience than any of the others I had spoken with. He was easy to talk to, and he was able to properly diagnose me with posttraumatic stress disorder (PTSD). I started to do research on the subject of PTSD, which helped me to understand what I was going through and the symptoms associated with it: loss of memory, forgetting things I wanted to remember, and remembering things I wanted to forget. Once I learned to trust my new psychologist, I could tell him anything. There were so many questions I had. I would write down my questions in my journal and, at my weekly appointments, would go over the week before with him. The nightmares, trembling, rapid heartbeat, alarming feelings; (especially if I heard sirens), and the headaches were all symptoms of PTSD. Every week, there seemed to be a new challenge. I felt at times I was losing my mind. The only thing that kept me grounded was my psychologist telling me it was normal for what I was going through! He wanted me to see a psychiatrist early on in my treatment with him, but out of pride, I refused. Every time I went to his office, I was able to walk out knowing, for what I was going though, I was normal, suffering from PTSD and experiencing a wide range of symptoms, which not only effected me psychologically and spiritually but physically as well, but I was normal for the situation I was in.

In the early fall of 2004, I received a letter from the attorney representing the family of the man who died in the accident. The letter stated that I needed to send that notice to my insurance company. I realized the family was suing my insurance company. The trauma of that itself was overwhelming; in my mind I thought the family had forgiven me. My psychologist was a great help to me during this time. Throughout the "lawsuit" process—meeting with an attorney, which my insurance company assigned to me, and the deposition, which was a nightmare itself—my psychologist was a sounding board of understanding and empathy, as well as a man of God with wisdom, which I needed the most of at the time. Throughout this process, he reassured me that the family had forgiven me, but they were also were entitled to money under my policy and under law for their loss. It is not that I didn't want them to receive any money; it was my need to know I was forgiven that was more important to me at that time.

Also, the youth pastor at my church, Pastor Scott Durbin, was a great encouragement to me. I could go in and talk to him about everything that was going on, and he always accepted me and continued to remind me not only of God's forgiveness but of the family of the man who died.

One day I remember feeling so down about myself I was almost to the point of arguing with the church's worship leader who is also my friend, Joel. I was feeling like a terrible person and I had him raise his right hand and tell me he didn't feel any different toward me then as he did before the accident. I had this stigma that I was no longer a good person and everybody around me should think I was a bad person. I was trying hard to come to terms with the accident itself, missing the opportunity to tell the man's son I was sorry, and then the lawsuit; my plate was full and I was overloaded.

I felt like I was back at square one again in my emotional healing process. My close friends would listen to me over and over as I talked about the same things over and over. My brother and sister were the same way. My brother would call to check on me, and my sister would come every week to take me to the store or do errands. My brother even put me on his cell phone package so if I was out and about and needed anything, I could call him. Everyone around me was a great encouragement to me, but I was still beating myself up on the inside. My psychologist gave me a scenario of priests who actually whipped themselves so they could experience the same type of torment Jesus went through. He was right; I was tormenting myself, but I felt I deserved it.

It wasn't long after I started counseling that I had a feeling I should visit the grave of the man who died in the accident. My psychologist wouldn't agree or disagree with me; he wanted me to make the decision on my own. I called my friend Judy, and we did some research and found out where he was buried. She came and picked me up and drove me to the cemetery. I had bought a small plant and had written a card to the man who died. When we got to the cemetery, Judy drove slowly as we looked for his name on a gravestone. When I saw it I said, "There it is!" Judy stopped and told me she would give me some time to myself and she would be back in a little while. As she drove off, I walked slowly toward his gravesite. Once there I knelt down. I noticed right away he was a University of Michigan fan because there was an emblem on his tombstone; it was colored so it stood out. He had a child, who had died years before, who was buried next to him. My mind was open, but my heart was numb. The date of the accident, May 29, 2004, was there in big letters. I began to dig a small hole for the flowers I brought. I then weeded around his gravestone. I wanted so much to talk to him, but he wasn't there. After a few minutes of just sitting there, I was surprised I was not crying and actually felt guilty I wasn't. When I stood up, the song by the group Casting Crowns, off their CD *The Altar and the Door*, entitled "East to West" came to my mind. The song says, "Jesus can you show me just how far the east is from the west, 'cause I can't bear to see the man I've been come rising up in me again. In the arms of your mercy I find rest, 'cause you know just how far the east is from the west, from one scarred hand to another." The song signifies God's amazing grace and how he forgets our sins and failures and never measures them. From my perspective, at that moment in my life, east to west was six feet deep.

As I walked away from the grave, the question, "Is this real?" came to my mind. From what I had just seen, there was now no doubt that I had killed someone.

I started to walk toward the road, and within a couple of minutes, Judy pulled up. The thought crossed my mind that it was pretty good timing on her part. As we pulled away, I said to Judy, "I couldn't tell him I was sorry because he wasn't there."

(Years later, Judy told me the whole time I was there, she never took her eyes off me.)

Chapter Four

The other side of the Fence

I read many books throughout this time, doing research on stress and guilt and how to overcome them. My psychologist wanted me to read a book entitled *A Grace Disguised* by Jerry Sittser. I immediately went to the store to get the book. I didn't make it through the first chapter; I had to put it down. The book is a true story of how a man dealt with a traumatic tragedy. His family had been in a car accident, victims of a drunk driver. Mr. Sittser lost his third-born child, his wife, and his mother. He and his other three children survived the accident, but one of them suffered a severe injury to his leg.

As I started to read the book, I was in tears, for the details the author laid out were overwhelming by any person's standpoint. From mine I felt like I was the one who had killed the members of his family.

On my next appointment with my psychologist, I took the book with me, having a secret desire to hit him with it! I was angry at him and asked in tears, "Why would you want me to read such a book? I am feeling like I was the one who hurt him and his family." My psychologist explained he wanted me to realize what I was going through was "loss and grief." Although from a different perspective, it was a loss. He challenged me to read the book, as hard as it was for me to do so, and flag every emotion Mr. Sittser felt if I too was experiencing the same emotion. I did read the book. It now looks like an accordion, as it is stuffed with sticky notes and colored tabs throughout it. Although I refer to it as "being on the other side of the fence," I related to him and the losses he and his family suffered. My psychologist and I would talk in detail about the book and how loss is loss and grief is grief. It can be overwhelming. This book gave me great hope even though I was on the other side of the fence. I was able to start healing emotionally and spiritually as I read it.

Chapter Five

God Reached out to Me

The people who surrounded me continued to love me in spite of the depression and overwhelming survivor's guilt I suffered. Months passed and it was close to a year since the accident had happened. My heart was heavy with grief as I tried so hard not to think about the accident and everything that had happened, but it truly consumed me. The day came and went with nothing standing out as significant to me, other than the fact that I cried most of the day and could not think of anything else but the accident and everything that had happened since. As the week rolled on, I made plans with friends to have them pick me up and take me with them to an open house I had been invited to. It was for Brittany, a young friend who had just graduated from high school. I had to go!

Brittany is one of my heroes. When I first met her, she was three years old and bound to a wheelchair, and now she was able to walk and was making plans to go to college. I couldn't miss her celebration. When I arrived at the open house, I again ran into Liz, an old friend whom I had just ran into and spoken briefly with a week earlier. We happened to be at the hospital at the same time. She was just finishing up taking her husband to an appointment, and I was just getting there to see my neurologist. Liz approached me at the open house and handed me an envelope. I went to my friends' van, the ones who drove to the open house, and read the following:

> Dear Linda,
> As I was reading from one of my devotional books this morning (*Quiet Moments with God*) I thought of you and our conversation a week ago. I hope that it will be encouraging to you too. You are in my prayers and I pray today that something new and special will be brought into your life. I am reminded of the song, "I just feel like something good is about to happen. I just feel like something good is on it's way. He has promised that he'd open all of heaven and brother it could happen any day. When God's people humble themselves and call on Jesus and look to heaven expecting as the pray." I just feel like something good is about to happened and sister this could be that very day!
>
> Love,
> Liz

As I went on to read the devotion she had copied from her book, I noticed right away the date was

May 29, the date of the accident. I started to read the article that followed:

> "Come and see the works of God; He is awesome in His doing toward the sons of men" (Psalm 66:5).
>
> Dear God, today I want to let go of my hurting memories of the past. I accept your forgiveness and want to forgive everything and everyone in the past—including myself. Thank you that you deliberately forgot my failures, but never forgot me. You tell me what not to remember and why. "Do not remember the former things, nor consider the things of old. Behold, I will do a new thing, now it shall spring forth; shall you not know it?" (Isaiah 43:18-19). Lord, I forget the past by remembering you. I remember that you are willing to forget my sins and failures. I confess them specifically. At your command, I move through the prison of my memories, leading out each captive memory for display before You. You have said, "I even I, am He who blots out your transgressions for My own sake; and I will not remember you sins . . . state your case, that you may be acquitted" (Isaiah 43:25-26).
>
> In response I bring all my hurting memories into the court of Your presence. I'm astounded: As I finish my condemnatory judgment on myself, I hear Your voice

sound in my soul, I forgot that long ago;
now you are free to forget it. *

As I finished the article, the tears were streaming down my face and as I looked up, my eyes came across the clock in the van, and I realized the time was the time of the accident the year before. I cried even harder. I was amazed that Liz remembered the anniversary of the accident because we were not that close.

Once I got myself together, I went and sat down by Liz, with my sunglasses on so no one could see my tears. I told her I had read the note. She started to tell me how the Lord had put me in her heart from the start of the morning of the 29th, and she had tried to call me but I didn't answer. She said she felt strongly that the Lord wanted her to give the card to me today, so she copied it and brought it with her. As I sat there looking at her, I was even more amazed she remembered the anniversary of the accident; with a look of surprise on her face she said, "I didn't know that!"

We both started to cry and we sat and talked about how precious God is when He wants to get our attention and to give us a message.

I was amazed at the fact that I truly felt God had moved in my heart that day, but I have to be honest and say that I asked Him, "If you were here today, where were you a year ago?"

---

* Used with permission see Biblography

Chapter Six

How can God use me Again?

One of the things I remember about this time was always being scared of what was coming and how I was going to deal with it. I discovered during this time I would start to worry about things before I needed to. I put a lot of brain power or emotional energy into worrying about something that hadn't even happen yet, thus making the situation more difficult than what it was. I didn't know what to do with myself. The nightmares were the worst: waking up, being scared out of my mind, but not knowing of what. I started to have a recurring nightmare about the accident but they were very foggy nightmares. I was being taken out of my car and saw a vision of a car on its side. This nightmare continued and I would wake up very scared. I found out through my brother that the car in my nightmare fit the description of the car I had hit. I must have started to come out of the seizure while they were taking me out of my car, but the trauma of the accident wouldn't let me remember it until months later. It never turned into a clear dream; it was always foggy, yet the accident didn't happen on a foggy day.

One night I was staying with my friends Lorrie and Mark. I was sleeping in one of their girls' rooms by myself. I had a terrible nightmare and was very shaken up. I went into Mark and Lorrie's room and walked to Lorrie's side of the bed. I woke her up, and she could tell I was shaken. She scooted over toward her husband and told me to lie down next to her. She held on to me, saying, "It's going to be okay, and you are going to get through this. You are not alone!" I fell into one of the most peaceful sleeps I had since the accident. In the morning, I woke up but was back in the girl's room; I thought I must have gotten up at one point and gone back to the girls' room. Downstairs, I questioned Lorrie about this, asking, "Did I wake you up last night?" She replied, "No."

It was all a dream. A terrible nightmare followed by a beautiful dream in which my friend held on to me, helping me to feel safe in spite of my fear. Although I had bad dreams after that, I never experienced another traumatic dream like the one that night. God used Lorrie, someone I loved and trusted and someone who loved me back, in a dream. I believe now it was Jesus who was holding on to me; but with where I was at that point in my life, I wouldn't have trusted Him, so He used Lorrie, and she was sound asleep the whole time.

I felt I couldn't work but knew I needed to do something to help me move forward. I began to volunteer at the Genesee County Free Medical Clinic. I had volunteered there before, but this time was different, my confidence was gone, I literally had to start from the bottom. I couldn't drive, so Carolyn, the clinic coordinator, would come and pick me up, usually on Friday. I worked with a lady named Rose at the front desk where we greeted people and checked them in. Rose was a great comfort to me. I felt I couldn't screw anything up or hurt anybody since she was there. Even though I volunteered just a few hours a week, I was exhausted when I got home. But I felt it kept my head above water by having a sense of helping others even though I was struggling to help myself.

One day I couldn't find a file for a patient. I looked high and low for it. I then went to the director of the clinic and asked for her assistance. She came to the reception area, walked over to a stack of files, and found the file I had been looking for, which was only about four files down. I thanked her, handed the file to a nurse, and took a break. I went outside, crying my eyes out. I was saying to myself, "You can't even find a single file. How in the world are you ever going to find a decent job again?" I don't know how long this pity party lasted, but before long, Bill, Carolyn's husband, pulled up and noticed me.

Jokingly he asked, "Are you holding up the wall?" "Yes," I answered. It was a couple of minutes later that Carolyn came out and approached me with concern. She looked down at me and asked, "Did you have a seizure?" I said, "No, I couldn't find a file!" I can't remember her exact words but she wasn't happy with me. I guess someone noticed I was missing and the staff of the clinic started to look for me, thinking I was having a seizure somewhere. It was a busy place and the last thing they needed was to be looking for me. Carolyn had Bill take me home. I felt like such a failure.

It was the fall of 2005, and Hurricane Katrina had hit the Southern Coast of the United States hard. Our church was forming a work team to go down and help with disaster relief. Since I had been on five mission trips before the accident and wasn't working, I felt I should go. But Pastor David wanted me to get permission from my psychologist to go. My psychologist and I spoke about it, and I began to realize that maybe this would be too overwhelming for me under the circumstances I was all ready enduring. So I decided it would be best not to go.

It was also during this time that I became a patient at the Genesee County Free Medical Clinic. I didn't have insurance and I wasn't happy with my neurologist. Although I am not a doctor, I know my body and felt, after I had the seizure at the restaurant and my neurologist prescribed another seizure medicine, that it was that medicine and having too much of it that caused the seizure that caused the accident. I had numerous seizures after the accident; and every time I had one, he would increase the dose of the second medication, which made things even worse for me. It was too much medicine and not the right kind of medicine for me.

The free clinic arranged for me to be seen by another neurologist. The first time I saw him, he asked me, "Do you think these medicines are helping you?"

I said, "Sir, not only did they kill someone else, they are killing me!"

He said, "Well, we need to change that!" He set up a plan to get me off the two seizure medications I was on and try a whole new one. It was rough for about three months as my body adjusted to the change, but it worked!

I felt that doctor cared a great deal for his patients and his willingness to listen to my opinion and set up a goal plan saved my life, for I was physically and emotionally at wits' end. Once I did get on a community health plan, I was so excited because he was now going to get paid for treating me. I remember when I went in after I got insurance and told him, "I have insurance now!" He said, "Good for you!" It didn't faze him a bit. His focus was on getting me back on my feet, not on money. He continues to be my neurologist and unfortunately, now that I am well, I only get to see him once a year. But God chose him and He chose the best for me!

I also found my own primary care physician who was very cautious when prescribing medicines for me because of my seizure disorder. I like that about him. He doesn't just throw prescriptions at me. We work together and I am comfortable with his care and his concern.

Chapter Seven

Overcoming Mountains

In November 2005, my friend Sally, who is a certified registered nurse anesthetist, invited me to visit her in Alaska. She was there as a contracted anesthetist, working at a small hospital on the island of Sitka. She said if I could afford the airfare, she would take care of everything else. I checked into airfare, and it was expensive. When I first called the airline, they said I couldn't use my accumulated points from all my mission trips to fly to Alaska. But I called the next day to see if I could get even a discount with my miles. That phone call turned out to be a winner. I got one of the best customer service representatives alive. She not only told me I could use my points but arranged for my trip and everything.

I was scared to fly alone. This was weird because I had so much experience in traveling, mostly internationally, that flying to another state shouldn't have bothered me, but it did. I was concerned I would have a seizure and cause a big hassle somewhere. But I wanted to go so badly, and Sally was determined to have me come. So I packed my bags and took off for Alaska. The trip was long, and I have never been able to sleep on planes. I remember the enormous relief I felt when I got to the Sitka airport, rounded the corner, and saw Sally. I had made it, and I was now safe with my friend. Sally had to work during the week, but I had her cell number if I needed anything. When she was off duty, she had a pager and had to be within twenty minutes of the hospital at all times. So, when she was working, I walked around the island several times and visited different places. Although it is a major port for cruise ships, it was the off-season, and many of the businesses were closed. But there was a lot of history there, and I explored every bit of it. It was the first time since the accident I was on my own. The island is beautiful. It is surrounded by mountains and it even has a small 2,550-foot mountain on the island called Mount Verstovia. I kept looking at it and wondered what it would be like to climb it.

    I loved the evenings after Sally got out of work. We would sit and have dinner and talk, or walk or just relax. I began to express to Sally my desire to climb Mount Verstovia, so she arranged for her neighbor Craig, a national forestry ranger, to drop me off at the base of the mountain. I was armed with a can of bear spray, a hiking stick, two bottles of water, an extra pair of gloves, a scarf, and Sally's cell phone, all stuffed into a back pack. Craig told me it takes him twenty minutes to climb the mountain; I figured it was going to be an exciting adventure that would take about an hour or so. It turned out to be one of the hardest things I have ever done.

Not too long into my adventure, I started asking myself, "Why did I want to climb this mountain?" I was beginning to think I really was crazy. But as I grew more tired, I also grew more and more determined—determined not to quit. Quitting wasn't an option. I imagined some of my friends climbing with me—people who had lifted me up when I was down, people who had been there for me. I remember the people who had said they would pray for me. I had to keep going for those people. It gave me strength to think of them.

I also thought about the man who died in the accident and wondered if he ever got a chance to climb a mountain since his life was cut short. I needed to continue on for him.

As I continued to climb, it became muddier and more slippery. There were a few places where there was rope already hooked around trees, which I used to pull myself up over rocks or difficult places to climb. There were two places where cable was attached to the mountain itself, and I hung onto those while I was working my way around cliffs. It seemed like the mountain was getting steeper and steeper as I continued to climb. I was starting to see frost on things, then it started to snow. It was a different type of snow than I can ever remembering seeing. It was white but also heavier, a cross between a big raindrop and a snowflake. I was becoming exhausted, but I continued to climb. One of the most flustering things I found out about forest-mountain climbing is just like things I was finding out about life: you can't see what's coming. You know it's there but you can't see what's around the next corner. It seemed I started to climb straight up. I could see the trees coming to an end so I knew I was getting to the top, but the trail just kept going up and up. I was getting discouraged. Then Sally's cell phone rang; it was her calling from the apartment. She asked where I was. I told her I thought I was near the top, and she said to give her a call once I got up there. So I had to keep going. It seemed as though the trees were getting thinner as I looked up, yet the trail just kept going and going. But then, as I made a turn and climbed through a few more trees and up a few more rocks, I realized, as I got closer, that it was the lookout over the town and port of Sitka; I had made it to the top of the mountain! I immediately saw a small bench there, which I used for its purpose—rest! I enjoyed looking out over the town and port of the island; it was beautiful. I was thinking of how tired I was, asking myself if it was worth it. There were several postcards with the same image on them, and I could have gotten the same picture for twenty cents after a ten-minute walk to the store with no climbing!

It took me three hours to climb the mountain. I called Sally to let her know I had reached the top, and she said, "I am very proud of you!" It had been a long time since I heard someone tell me that. Maybe others had said it, but I didn't believe it, so I didn't hear it like I should have. But now I had something to be proud of. Now I had climbed a mountain!

I didn't stay too long at the top. I was tired, out of water, and hungry, so I started to climb down. The rocks were like ice and the ground was snowy.

My feet were already hurting. I noticed right away the pressure was now on my toes, as my body weight was now resting at the tip of my shoes, and I was slanting downward all the time. I knew it wouldn't take me as long to go down as it did to climb up. The trail was icy and with the rocks and downed timbers made it even more difficult. It seemed, with every step, like I would slide a bit. Coming to an area where I didn't see a safe step so for the sake of not slipping I decided to sidestep the trail. I took a few steps then before I had a chance to take a breath, the ground gave way and I fell, or I should say, bounced, head over heels roughly fifteen feet down the mountain. When I came to rest, I was looking up. And thought for sure I was dead, I moved just a bit and realized, because of pain, I was still alive! Sally's voice came to mind, "Whatever you do, stay on the trail, don't go off the trail!"

It took a few moments for me to register any emotion at all, but then I started to cry and shake, the "Linda Syndrome." Maybe I should now rename the "Linda Syndrome," to "Rolling Off the Mountain Syndrome" (ROTMS), pronounced "rootems." It took a few minutes for me to calm myself down enough to call Sally, who had me run my hands over my head and body to look for blood. I saw very little blood but had a goose egg the size of a pear on the right side of my head. Sally said, "As long as you're not bleeding, you need to get up and start climbing down again." Some may think that was very insensitive of her, but looking back, I believe it was exactly what I needed at that time. I needed someone to say,

"It's okay, and your are okay. Get up!" She said to call her again if I had any trouble and to call her when I got halfway down the mountain.

I kept asking myself over and over, "Why did I do this? Why did I climb a two-thousand-foot mountain?" Once I could see that I was about halfway down, I called Sally, who said she would start out and meet up with me on the trail. I took a short break and then was off again. Once I came upon her, I had the same feeling I had at the airport in Sitka and with Debbie after the seizure while buying shoes, I had found my friend! I finally made it off the mountain and crawled into Sally's car to go back to her apartment. I was able to take a shower and get the rocks and trees out of my hair. When I was done in the shower, I had to clean out the drain because of all the little twigs, leaves, and little rocks that had formed at the end of the tub. I did an examination of my body to see where else there was damage. The examination came out good. In spite of my "bounce," I had made it off the mountain with only a goose egg on my head, a very sore left shoulder, numerous bruises, and three scratches to my face.

Morning came too early the next day. Although I had slept well, my body was feeling the effects of the workout it had gotten the day before. It seemed like every muscle I knew I had had grown another muscle, which I had no idea was there. Even drinking a cup of tea was an alarming experience. Lifting the cup required all of the muscles in my arm, then those going up to my shoulder, then those down to my hip. Walking was difficult as I had to move one side of my body then move the other side. It was like walking with a stick up my bottom (that thought of maybe something actually being up there crossed my mind), but I thought I would be going beyond the friendship zone by asking my friend, even though she was a nurse, to check my bottom for me.

My Alaska adventure turned out to be a turning point for me. Things seemed to be easier after that as I came upon a situation that was difficult. I remembered I was a mountain climber. I had overcome something that was bigger than I ever imagined I could endure, but I did it! I was one who didn't give up. I had overcome a mountain, but as I looked forward, I knew I had much more to overcome.

Chapter Eight

Missing a chance to help my Brother

I was still having a hard time whenever I was out and saw an accident. I had to close my eyes or turn away. This worked well for me—out of sight, out of mind. One Friday night my friend Berta and I were driving and came upon what looked to be an accident about a quarter mile up the road. I closed my eyes immediately, and as we drew closer, I started asking Berta questions, "Do they need help? Do we need to call 911?" She said the police were already there, and it looked like everything and everybody was okay. We actually had to stop at the stoplight and wait, which made us not more the twenty feet from where the cars involved in the accident were. Once we turned the corner, Berta said it was okay to open my eyes. Even though my heartbeat was very fast and my breathing was a little off, I dealt with it. Two days later, my brother, Tom, called and said he needed to tell me something before I saw him again. He then began to tell me that he and my three-year-old autistic nephew, Chucky, were okay, but they were in an accident Friday night.

I asked him where, and then I asked him what time. It was them.

That was the accident I had closed my eyes to. As my brother was telling me this, I started to cry and shake, then I started to tell him, "I was right there. I could have stopped to help you!" He then said something to me that turned out to be another turning point in my healing process; he said, "Linda, if you had stopped and were reacting Friday night like you are reacting now, you would have been no help to me. Chucky was having a hard time, the lady in the other car was having a hard time, and I was dealing with the whole situation. To have you come up crying and all shaken up would have made the situation worse!"

I was truly thankful to the Lord that no one was hurt in the accident although my brother's car was badly damaged; the lady had made a turn right in front of him. But I had missed an opportunity to be there for my brother, one who has been there for me since day one of my seizures and the accident I was in.

I had to make a change and start to deal, little by little, with every fender bender, ambulance, and police car I came across. I began to keep my eyes open. Yes, my heart rate would get so high I thought my heart would pump out of my chest, but I kept my eyes open.

A few weeks later, I was riding my bike on the sidewalk near the grocery store. As I was approaching the intersection, I saw two cars, one jumping the light, slam into each other right before my eyes. My heart rate went up, and I started to shake. But I also started talking to myself, telling myself, "I can help. I used to be an instructor for the American Red Cross. I know basic first aid, I have a cell phone, I can help!" I put down my bike and walked into the intersection where traffic had stopped and asked one of the ladies if she was okay, and although shaken, she said she wasn't hurt. I walked alongside her damaged car as she drove it into a near by parking lot. The other lady walked from her car, and we all met up and took account that neither of them was hurt. I got out my cell phone and called 911, reporting to them a non-injury accident. When I hung up, one of the ladies asked if she could use my phone. As I handed it to her, it was then that the ladies noticed how shook up I was. I was actually shaking so badly the lady who had asked to use my phone had to hold my arm first, then take the phone with her other hand. I was embarrassed! An officer arrived just moments later, and I left the scene knowing I had done everything I could do. I had a good feeling, a feeling that reminded me of being on the mountain. In spite of what I considered an overwhelming circumstance, God used me even in my weaknesses. I walked away from that accident knowing I was on my way to overcoming an obstacle, which had been standing in my way for a long time—the obstacle of fear!

Chapter Nine

Stepping back into Life

It was the summer of 2006, almost two years after the accident, when one day my friend Jodi stopped by and said she wanted to talk to me. As we sat down, she said she wanted me to call someone. Her husband, Jason, had been in a major car accident the day before Thanksgiving in 2003. They had been through a tough time. Jodi told me they hired a case manager named Elizabeth, who helps them with all kinds of things, but mostly getting the best treatment and help with the insurance company. I called her and we met.

Immediately Elizabeth set up an appointment with a neuropsychiatricst, someone who not only deals with neurology disorders but also psychiatry. He was able to prescribe medicines for me, which helped with the nightmares, depression, and overwhelming anxiety, without the threat of seizures. Adapting to these medicines was challenging, but little by little, I started to feel maybe God still had something more for me.

Elizabeth was a great help and comfort to me throughout this time in my life. She challenged me in many ways. One was to find work again. But to do that, I would need to drive again. This was another mountain for me. How could I drive again with what had happened? We got a prescription from my neuropsychiartrist for driving rehabilitation.

I remember starting out to drive again, and it was hard. Although my driving rehabilitation instructor was a nice guy and he had his own brake pedal in case I screwed up, I was beyond nervous. I was white-knuckled behind the steering wheel, and every muscle in my body would tense up. This caused me to experience migraine headaches and muscle spasms. Each session only lasted an hour, but at the end of that hour, I was exhausted because of all the brain and emotional power it took to drive again. I would have to take a nap after every session. It was also at this time that Elizabeth got me into massage therapy. It helped a great deal with the muscle spasms and migraines. Little by little, I was gaining confidence. My driver rehabilitation specialist never had to grab the wheel or hit the brake pedal for me. I also started to look for a used car for when I would be able to drive again. My friend Dennie actually found the car. Dennie and our friend Gary took me to see the car, and I had Dennie do most of the talking with the seller. He let us take a test drive, and Dennie took me down a side road where I could drive the car. I liked it. It had low miles and looked in pretty good condition. I had been saving for a car since I started to work with Elizabeth, who had given me a vision to get back on my feet again. I called my brother Tom and talked to him about the car, and after he and Dennie talked, I decided to buy it. Gary had to drive my new car back to my apartment for me since I was not a licensed driver.

I was a good driver before the accident; the first accident I was in was not my fault, a lady crossed the center line and hit me head-on because she was swatting at a bee inside of her truck. I had to learn not to fear being behind the wheel again. I was within two weeks of "graduating" from driver rehab. I had been practicing with my friend Berta. She would come over and pick me up, and then we would go to parking lots so I could practice with her car. She was going to let me use her car to take my state exam to get my license back. I was excited but somewhat apprehensive.

I had been asked to speak at the Deeper Life Women's Retreat to do a workshop on my experiences since the accident. I didn't have much experience in doing any type of public speaking, so I set up a pre-workshop workshop. I invited about fifty people to come and hear my presentation. I handed out feedback forms and was able to make appropriate changes to my presentation based on the feedback. All of it was good! It was refreshing to know I was on the right track. Right about that time I saw an advertisement to get a big discount to switch to another pharmacy. I took advantage of the advertisement and received twenty-five dollars for switching. But with that switch came a change in the generic version of one of my medicines, and I wound up having a seizure! I was with friends having dinner and listening to a presentation by missionaries. I got up to go to the bathroom, and when I went to go back in, they were doing a closing prayer so I stayed outside the doors and started looking at the missionaries' display. The next thing I remember was my friend Janet looking down at me, telling me she was there and it was going to be okay. That seizure was a grand mal and I wound up being taken to the hospital. Janet had called my brother, for I wear a medical ID tag with his and my sister's phone numbers on it. My brother Tom came, again, to the hospital and stayed with me, again, as a doctor put staples in my head because of a large gash caused from the impact when I hit the floor. I had a concussion and had to work with my new neurologist for about three months to get my equilibrium straight again.

Of course, this put driving on hold, again! But with my equilibrium being off, I didn't feel like driving anyway. I was dizzy all the time, and with dizziness came all kinds of side effects. I even had to hold on to friends and family as I walked around.

I still had my commitment to the Deeper Life Retreat and knew I would need special help. I contacted my friends, Berta, Judy, and Melissa, and asked them if they would go with me to assist me. Although I was able to get through both workshops I was scheduled to present, I was exhausted by the end of the day. My friends never left me alone. One of them was always with me.

I realized the generic version of that drug was why I had this seizure. From there, my neuropsychitrist made out the prescription to be DAW, which means "Dispense as Written," meaning no generics. I have not had a seizure since!

I was able to try driver rehabilitation again after six months. I had to go with a new driver rehabilitation specialist because the one I did have no longer did rehab. That made me very nervous. He had a different car and I needed to adapt to it. I continued to receive massage therapy as all the symptoms I had during my first round of driver rehab resurfaced. I didn't give up and was able to pass all the tests and graduate and get my license back in April of 2007, but my psychologist wanted a restriction on my license, limiting me to no night driving. I was okay with that. But then Elizabeth and I worked on finding a job for me; that was when I ran into a problem. I received an opportunity to interview at Peckham Inc. in Lansing, Michigan. Their main goal is to get people rehabilitated and back into the workforce. I interviewed with Matt June, manager of business services. The job was for the call center, where I would be a customer service representative. I was so nervous when I interviewed with him, but I told him, "Sir, if you will put me at bat, I will swing!" I didn't promise him a home run; I promised I would swing. At that time, I didn't have the confidence to do what I had done before, but I was willing to try anything to get going again

Mr. June called a couple of days later and said he had a position open for me, but it was for a second shift position. I told him I would have to work it out with my doctors to see if I could get the restriction for nighttime driving removed. My psychologist stood firm and said, "No!" I really liked the guy before that! I argued with him and told him that this was an opportunity I had to take advantage of, but he remained firm. All my other physicians released me except for him. "Everybody else thinks I am okay, it's just you!" He didn't change his mind even after tears, tears, and more tears.

I reluctantly called Mr. June back and told him I couldn't get the restriction removed. He said he would keep me in mind if anything became open during the day or to let him know when the restriction was removed.

I can't ever remember being so mad at my psychologist before, feeling he was being unreasonable. The accident didn't even happen at night; it happened in the late afternoon. But he wanted me to get some more experience behind the wheel before I started to drive at night. This guy had walked through hell and then led me back out, but I was so mad at him. But I knew God had placed him in my life for a reason, and I didn't want to go around him to get his decision overridden because of the fact that God had placed him in my life. So, as mad as I was, I had to surrender the anger (sigh) and go with the flow.

Two weeks later, Mr. June called to say there was a day shift position that opened up. I got the job! I was able to drive to Lansing, Michigan, from Flint, Michigan. I left for work just after the sun rose and was able to return home long before it set. The restriction was finally removed about three months after I began driving again.

Chapter Ten

Nothing is going to happen to you without going through me First!

Early on in my work at Peckham Inc., it was stressful because of learning new things and wanting so much to do a good job. The stress of wanting to do a good job, I believe, actually was hindering me from doing the best I could do. Not that I did a poor job, but with constant worry hanging over my head, it didn't free my brain to relax and take in as much information as I believe it was capable of handling. I tried stress relief tactics like deep breathing, stretching, and taking walks around the building at break time, which all helped but never completely took away the fear of screwing up and losing my job. One day in particular, when I was stressed out, I went to my direct supervisor, Jason, who said to me something that was another turning point for me.

I can't remember exactly what I went to him for, but I am sure it had to do with me being shook up about trying to do a good job and worrying what would happen to me if I screwed up. He said,

"Nothing is going to happen to you without going through me first!" I'm not quite sure what it was about his statement. Jason is a former army police officer and is strong in both spirit and honor. Jason always respected me in spite of my anxiety and weaknesses and took time for me when I needed it. So my respect for him was immense. I don't know what it was about what he said; maybe it was the way he said it, firm and without hesitation. Maybe it was the way he looked at me when he said it—straight in the eyes without blinking. But his words and actions gave me a sense of peace that I hadn't experienced in a long time.

As my shift ended and I walked to my car, I said to myself, "If I could only use that statement as if Jesus was saying it to me, 'Nothing is going to happen to you without going through me first.' If I could just sense that peace about my life, knowing that nothing was going to happen to me that didn't go through Jesus first." In spite of everything I had gone through, I could overcome much of my anxiety and get on with my life.

But then I thought back to the day of the accident and wondered where He was when that happened! How could I trust Him after He let that pass through Him and basically approved it, just as He had with Job? The Bible says in Job 1:8, "Then the Lord said to Satan, 'Have you considered my servant Job?'" With that, Satan ran and made turmoil out of Job's life, and God knew the whole time what was going on. Job didn't even do anything wrong. I made a mistake and should have checked with my doctor before I drove again. Job lost everything! His family, his fortune, his health, yet he still trusted God. I had been so mad at Him since the accident, having a hard time trusting Him with anything, yet I knew I didn't want to go on with my life without Him. It was like riding a teeter-totter, up and down, wanting to serve Him but not wanting any pain or anguish. The accident didn't shock God off is throne; He knew of it. I have to stop and take a deep breath as I ponder that thought, He knew of it! My God, the one I loved, trusted, and served, allowed it to pass through Him and come to me. In the Bible, David, in Psalms 32:7, writes to God, "You are my hiding place; you will protect me from trouble and surround me with songs of deliverance." David, although a king, screwed up royally throughout his life, but God delivered Him and provided peace for him in times of trouble.

As I look back on the day Jason spoke those words to me, I have to thank God for continuing to look out for me although I screwed up. I thank Him for being strong for me when I am weak, for looking me in the eye through His word and for promising to surround me with "songs of deliverance" in times I am in trouble.

Chapter Eleven

I don't deserve This!

After my work at Peckham began, I immediately began to think, because of gas prices, that I would need to move to Lansing, Michigan. The idea of being so far away from my family and friends was frightening. One of the first things I thought of was where I would go to church? I remembered one pastor, Doug Bradshaw from the East Michigan Conference of the Free Methodist church, and knew of his wife, Kathy. He pastors a church in Williamston, which is close to Lansing. I didn't know them well but decided to call him and get service times for the coming Sunday. He was very nice on the phone and said he would look forward to seeing me that Sunday. I did go to the church, and I walked out in tears. Not because I had a bad experience, but because I sensed God was calling me to move, and I was scared to do so. I started to check into apartments and wanted to get one as close to Peckham as possible just in case I had another seizure and would be able to walk to work. I found a nice apartment complex about one and a half miles from Peckham. God opened the door for me to get a great move-in deal on a one-bedroom apartment there, so I moved.

It was during this transition that I felt led to go back to the grave of the man who died. I didn't know why, but I just felt I should go. I took another plant. This time the tears came before I even knelt down. I was by myself and the cemetery was quiet. It was a beautiful late summer afternoon. I don't know how long I was there but I just started to talk to him like he was there. I told him how sorry I was for everything that had happened and that I would change places with him if I could because I didn't deserve all of the good things that were happening to me. I told him I prayed for his family and that I would continue to pray for them. I became paralyzed as I sat there. I just continued to sit there and could not stop crying. After some time I realized I needed some help, so I got out my cell phone and started from the top of my contact list. My first friend didn't not answer; the second friends were Bob and Debbie. When Bob answered, I told him I needed to talk with Debbie. He could tell I was shaken up. Debbie came to the phone and once I told her where I was, she asked, "Linda, why are you there?" I told her, "I wanted to tell him I was sorry, I never told him I was sorry the first time I came!" She began to talk to me to relieve my overwhelming feelings. I don't know how long we talked, but she got me back on my feet with her encouraging words. She talked to me until I stopped crying and told me to call her once I got home, and if I did start to cry again, she wanted me to pull over and call her again.

Once I got home and called Debbie back, I then began to write a letter. This letter was to the man's family. I had never apologized to them either. I wrote a long three-page letter explaining to them everything that had happened and that I was sorry. I called one of my friends and ran the letter by her; she said, "It's a beautiful letter but you don't need to tell them all of that. You can just let them know you are sorry!" So I wrote another letter. This one was two pages long. Then I remembered my friend's words and I wrote another letter. This was a simple four-sentence paragraph. That was the one I sent to the family's attorney and asked him to forward it to them. I do not know if they ever received it. I had done all I could to make amends for the loss I caused them. I had this feeling that I didn't deserve all of the good things that were happening to me.

Chapter Twelve

Still Overwhelming!

At work a few days later, we had a fire drill. The alarm for the fire drill was very loud and overwhelming for me. I sat at my desk and didn't know what to do. My mind went blank. As people were walking by me to exit the building I just sat there. Then Judy, one of my coworkers, stopped and said, "Linda, you need to aux out (a procedure to shut off my phone) and lock your computer; it's a fire alarm!" She helped me to aux out as I locked my computer and then we walked outside. My nervous system was in overdrive and I began to tremble and tried to fight off the tears. Judy hugged me and was talking to me, saying everything was ok and it was just a drill.

Just a few days after that on Friday, October 19, 2007, Williamston was hit by an F2 tornado. Many homes were damaged some destroyed. There were downed trees all over. There was even a couple who had lost their lives, their funeral was at our church.

On the way to church the Sunday after the tornado, I drove past people who were standing in the midst of the chaos that was once their homes. My heart was beating out of my chest and I was fighting back the tears. We had services that day though our church had limited electricity. Pastor Doug encouraged those who were able to come back that afternoon to help as they were able. I even stood up and emphasized the importance of teamwork and what a difference we could make by helping those in need by working as a team. When I arrived that afternoon, I went with a team under the leadership of Warren Bates. We went to a neighborhood that had sustained tremendous damage. When we got to the end of the street, Warren stopped the van. My heartbeat was up, my hands were shaking, and my breathing was off. I had to push myself to get out of the van. Although, I have good organizational skills, my mind was numb because of the devastation that surrounded us. Every place I looked at was damaged. I had to remember our objective to help where we could. As Warren and I approached a gentleman who was working in his yard, my nervousness was overwhelming. I took the lead just because I was so nervous and didn't know where to start. I introduced us and asked if we could help him. He got tears in his eyes. Warren never knew how shook up I was, and I didn't tell him because I barely knew him. We worked on the gentleman's yard for about four hours, making a big difference. He was so thankful. Although I was shaking and crying most of the time, I was able to cover it up. Warren or no one else knew I was freaking out on the inside. I took pictures of people in the church helping out that afternoon, hoping the church would use them to encourage teamwork in the future. About one hundred people from our church went to help that day. I had a good feeling about that, but my posttraumatic stress symptoms were surfacing and I was having a very hard time keeping them under control. I had a flashback of wanting to help with the Katrina relief effort, which, I then realized, would have been too overwhelming for me. And I appreciated the wisdom God gave Pastor David and my psychologist at the time I needed it the most.

That same week, my direct supervisor, who at the time was Eric, had passed out one day because of a change in his medicine. When they called 911, the fire department and paramedics showed up. The lights of the emergency units and seeing Eric, a man I respected a great deal, in so much pain was overwhelming. I sat at my desk, crying and shaking. I couldn't remove the situation from my mind.

I took the next day off because my posttraumatic stress symptoms were back. I couldn't sleep, I was shaking, my heart beat was up, and I was having a hard time just coping. Just like at the beginning after the accident, I was unsure of myself.

Eric returned to work the following Monday and was doing well. That helped calm me down a bit, but my PTSD symptoms persisted. I started to experience chest pains but ignored it, knowing that when I was shook up, the muscles in my body tighten. But the symptoms kept coming and going.

It was about two weeks after all the incidents leading up my PTSD symptoms resurfacing that I attended care group. Care groups are an extension of the church in which you can get to know a small group of people and learn to love, care, and help each other in times of need. My chest pain was immense that night. I was afraid to mention it to anyone because I knew they would probably want to call an ambulance. So I did one of the most stupid things I could have ever done at that time. I slipped out without anyone noticing me and drove myself to the hospital (so much for love, trust, and caring on my part). Once there, I was totally freaked out and called my pastor. I asked him to come. When he arrived, I just spilled my heart out to him. I told him the accident was my fault and if people in the church knew it was my fault, they would not like me very much. Pastor Doug held my hand and talked to me, saying, "Linda, it was an accident and you need to forgive yourself!" I am not sure how long he was there, but he stayed until my vital signs were normal. He has had so much experience at hospitals' bedsides that he knew how to read the machines. I was admitted, but even after numerous test, they found nothing wrong with me physically, which was good. But I had to deal with my PTSD being back, like a slap in the face.

My psychologist and I narrowed down why my symptoms resurfaced. The changes that I experienced, though good, were still changes, and change is stressful! In a very short time I had a new job, a new church, and a new place to live. Then we looked at the traumatic incidents of the fire alarm, the tornado, and Eric passing out. His reassurance that I was going to be okay was a great comfort to me.

It helped a great deal to be at Peckham inc. through out this time. All I had to do was to look up from my desk, and I could see many people who have had to overcome enormous obstacles to get to where they were at. Some even had their obstacles from birth. My friend and coworker, Staci, has cerebral palsy and has limited movement of her hands and arms. But that doesn't get in her way. She is a superb customer service representative and although bound to a wheelchair, the chair doesn't bind her. She is just one of the many heroes at Peckham Inc. who made me realize things could be worse for me. I have never heard her complain. Stories she has told me of when she was younger encouraged me. Like the one of her and friends going roller-skating; she already had her wheels! Then there was the day she was not able to get her driver's license. Her parents gave her fifteen minutes of "pity party" time and that was it. If I measured all of my "pity party" time because I couldn't drive, let's just say we would run out of measuring space.

Chapter Thirteen

Unchained!

On November 11, 2007, I went to church as I did every Sunday, still searching for purpose and for God. Pastor Doug gave a sermon on forgiveness. There was a pile of chains on the altar, chains of different colors and weights. The service started out as a married couple, Chuck and Marie Nicols, came out and did a skit. The skit was focused on them going through their separate list of things that they wanted to ask the other person's forgiveness for. As the list went on, the items on the list became harder to forgive. They started to challenge each other on what they could and couldn't forgive each other for. A person caped in a black shroud came out and started to put a chain around the couple. As the skit ended, they both walked off the stage with the chain attached to them; they were now dragging the weight of the chain.

As the service went on, a clip from the movie *The Last Sin Eater* was shown. The movie centers on a young girl who feels responsible for the death of her sister and how she wanted the Sin Eater to take away her sin. She finds the Sin Eater and goes through a ritual with him in which he pawns his own soul for the sins of the girl's. But after the ritual she realizes that nothing has changed; she still feels the same guilt. She then finds a traveling preacher who tells her about her about the only Sin Eater, Jesus!

She runs away in a glorious state because her pain has been removed. Full of immeasurable joy, she begins to run through a meadow. It reminded me of the day, April 25, 1986, when I asked Jesus to take away my sin.

As the service continued, I was thinking back at how I had put the chain on myself since the accident. Everyone else had forgiven me, but I had not forgiven myself or God. In his sermon, Pastor Doug gave numerous examples of how we hold back on offering forgiveness to people because we can use it against them; I visualized myself using my sin against myself because the circumstances of what happened weren't fair to others. I felt I should continue to punish myself because of the overwhelming forgiveness I received from the family of the man who died. You don't hear of people knocking on someone's door, saying, "We don't hold this against you!" It is unheard of! I had to be punished. I tried to get arrested but failed. But because I couldn't find anyone to punish me, I had to punish myself. I chose the chain that bound me for years. But the chain was heavy; it bore me down into a deep crater, which was dark and scary. The walls were too high to climb with the chain attached. I couldn't find a way out of it. As I sat there, I began to realize God never intended for me to wear that chain. He already made a provision long before I was born to remove my sin and mistakes by providing Jesus, but I had been so overwhelmed with tragedy of the accident I didn't see His grace or mercy. It was hard for me to believe God would forgive me for such a terrible mistake.

Then two people came forward and sang the song "East to West," the same song that came to mind the first time I went to the man's gravesite.

Again, I was physically numb as the service went on, but my heart and mind were open to God's plan. Pastor Doug then spoke about God not wanting anyone to walk out of the church that day dragging a chain. He also invited people to come pick a chain and throw it into the barrel as a symbol of God's forgiveness to them or forgiveness of another.

My heart began to hunger for my chain to be removed—the chain I had put on myself, I needed God's help to remove.

The worship team started to sing the worship style song, "Amazing Grace (My Chains Are Gone)." As people began to go forward, I was drawn to go up and get a chain. I tried to grab the biggest, ugliest, and dirtiest chain there was—I felt I didn't deserve anything more—but I couldn't get it out from beneath the pile. Marie Nicols who was there handed me a chain and said, "Use this One!" I stood up, stepped up on the stage, and with my back to the congregation, I looked at the chain. Several things came to my mind, but the one which was the most prevalent was the lack of trust I had in my heart for God for the last three and half years. Pastor Doug walked up to me and said, "Linda, are you ready to forgive yourself?" As I looked at the chain I thought for a moment and then I said, "Yes, but I need to do something first!" He didn't ask what.

I walked over the bridge on the stage that led to a cross, which was on the wall. As I laid my head on the foot of that cross, I didn't ask God to forgive me for the accident, for I had already asked Him to do that about one million times. Instead, I asked him to forgive me for the sins I had committed against Him since the accident, to forgive me for not trusting Him. I also thanked Him for providing so many people who had reached out to me and were His hands and feet over the past three and half years.

As I walked away from the cross, I approached the barrel and threw the chain in. I imagined Satan having to plug his ears because of the bang the chain made as it hit the barrel. I hoped it thundered through hell!

I then walked off the stage and down the aisle; my friend, Tim Alverson, was standing at the end of aisle. He is a tall guy, and he held out his arms to give me a big bear hug. I called it the "God hug," for I felt God was saying to me, "I've been waiting for this moment for a long time!"

I walked out of the church that day unchained for the first time in years. It felt good. God never intended for me to wear that chain. I chose it for myself and the enemy was elated for all those years and all those nightmares.

Since then I have committed myself to write my story to help others who wear chains, or know of someone who wears a chain, praying that God would give them wisdom to help the person in removing it. I also committed to myself to overcome any obstacles that stood in my way. Not too long ago, we had another fire alarm at work. This time all I needed was my coworker Karen saying, "Let's go!" It was amazing that I didn't cry and shake that time. I just needed a little "let's go," which is a major improvement from the last fire drill. I realized my chain was gone!

Epilogue

Looking back, it's amazing to me that I was feeling like my life was over and that God would never use me again. But throughout my experience as I was trying to heal, through every mistake, every weakness, every mountain and even the crater I encountered, God used me. His power was shown through it all. He did not let me stagnate in my faith, but He continued to bring fresh water to me through others, which I now want to use to refresh others.

As I continue in my quest to follow Christ, I have found the answer to my question that I asked my friend Linda the night of the accident, "How can God use this for His glory?" The answer was within me. Through the free will God has given to me and to you, we have to make a choice to turn the situations we encounter over to Him and see what He does with them. Most of this story centers on my weaknesses. But through my weakness, God has been magnified; my character and faith have been strengthened. God provided for me by simply walking with me; even though I was kicking and screaming at Him, He never let go.

I am not perfect, but He chose to use me just as He used people throughout history. If you look at a Bible, you will read of many people God used in spite of their weaknesses, failures, and fears. He continually called people to His side, but it was their choice to follow; and even after they started to follow and screwed up, He still loved them and used them, but there were consequences to all of their actions. His plan to magnify Himself through people may not be the way people want it to be. To walk with God is hard. I found that out through trauma and not understanding what He was doing when He was doing it. But I also had the wisdom to know that walking without Him was even harder. Even though I didn't know if I could trust Him anymore, I walked with Him because I knew I couldn't walk without Him. Even though I was mad at Him and verbalized my anger to Him numerous times and in various ways, I knew what life was like without Christ and I knew I couldn't walk away. I could have, but the relationship I have with God through Jesus is the most precious relationship I have ever encountered. I am so glad I never gave up on God, but most importantly, that He never gave up on me!

Although, I am still struggle with an anxiety disorder, progress is still being made in my life. God continues to use me. It has been a step by step process. I have overcome many obstacles and I know I will continue, with God's help, to overcome even more. I have found by looking fear in the face that life is worth living. God has so much for us. By seeking His will and asking

Him for His guidance and surrendering our will, He can and will use us even more than what we can imagine.

If you find yourself asking, "How can God use this for His Glory?" I encourage you to surrender whatever your situation is to God, and see what He does with it! P.S. Keep a journal, (He might lead you to write a book someday)!

If you would like to contact the author please e-mail her at: *mychainisgone@aol.com*

Bibliography

Chapter 3, Page 32
Stevenson, Mary, "Footprints in the Sand",
   (Copyright 1939)

Chapter 3 & 13, Page 36 & 77
Artist: Casting Crowns, CD: "The Altar and the Door", Song: East to West, Songwriter: Mark Hall, Beach Street Records, 2007

Chapter 4, Page 37
Sittser, Gerald, "A Grace Disguised: How the Soul Grows through Loss", 2nd Edition, (Zondervan, January 2005)

Chapter 5, Page 40
Taken from:
   Quiet Moments with God by Lloyd John Ogilvie
   Copyright © 2000 by Harvest House Publishers,
   Eugene, OR
   Used with Permission
   www.harvesthousepublishers.com

Chapter 13, Page 76
DVD: "The Last Sin Eater", Produced by Michael Landon, Jr., 20th Century Fox, 2007

Chapter 13, Page 77
Song writers: Thomlin, Chris; Giglio, Louie; Newton, John; Fettke, Tom; Traditional American Melody, "Amazing Grace (My Chains are Gone), Worship Together.com Songs, CCLI # 4768151, Cornerstone Church of Christ Worship Team", Copyright 2006

Scripture was taken from the HOLY BIBLE, NEW INTERNATIONAL VERSION ® Copyright © 1973, 1978, 1984 by International Bible Society. Used by permission of Zondervan Publishing House. All rights reserved.

Credits

Graphic Artist: Karen King

Back Cover Picture of Author:
Natural Image Photography, Burton, MI
www.naturalimages.biz

Hair Color: God

Hair Style: Kristin Bennett, Great Clips, Davison, MI

Makeup: Sandy Brown, Mary Kay Consultant, Flint, MI Sbrown11@marykay.co